A LifeGuid

BUSYNESS

Finding God in the Whirlwind

8 STUDIES FOR INDIVIDUALS OR GROUPS

Juanita Ryan

IVP Connect
An imprint of InterVarsity Press
Downers Grove, Illinois

InterVarsity Press
P.O. Box 1400, Downers Grove, IL 60515-1426
World Wide Web: www.ivpress.com
Email: email@ivpress.com

InterVarsity Press® is the book-publishing division of InterVarsity Christian Fellowship/USA®, a movement of students and faculty active on campus at hundreds of universities, colleges and schools of nursing in the United States of America, and a member movement of the International Fellowship of Evangelical Students. For information about local and regional activities, write Public Relations Dept., InterVarsity Christian Fellowship/USA, 6400 Schroeder Rd., P.O. Box 7895, Madison, WI 53707-7895, or visit the IVCF website at <www.intervarsity.org>.

While all stories in this book are true, some names and identifying information in this book have been changed to protect the privacy of the individuals involved.

Cover design: Cindy Kiple
Cover image: ©florintt/iStockphoto

ISBN 978-0-8308-3107-4 (print)
ISBN 978-0-8308-6425-6 (digital)

Printed in the United States of America ♾

As a member of the Green Press Initiative, InterVarsity Press is committed to protecting the environment and to the responsible use of natural resources. To learn more, visit greenpressinitiative.org.

P 20 19 18 17 16 15 14 13 12 11 10 9 8 7 6 5 4 3 2 1
Y 31 30 29 28 27 26 25 24 23 22 21 20 19 18 17 16 15

Contents

Getting the Most Out of *Busyness*

"How have you been?" a friend asks. "Busy," we say. And it is usually true. We are almost always busy.

For many of us much of our busyness is necessary to our survival or to our own and others' well-being. For some of us, our busyness may include activities of caring for or serving others.

But for many of us some portion of our busyness may also be self-imposed. We may get caught up in endless attempts to track and consume the information overload at our fingertips and on our many screens. Or we may be driven to achieve some form of status or success through long hours of working or tasking. Or we may be responding to internal and external pressures to gain approval from others or from God by doing or serving endlessly.

Both the good and necessary things in our lives and the self-imposed busyness of overdoing or overconsuming may be creating pressure and tension in our lives, robbing us of peace of mind and interfering with an awareness of God's presence with us. We may be left feeling empty, unfulfilled and hungry for spiritual nurture that will sustain us and guide us.

In the midst of the whirlwind of our lives, however, it may seem impossible to make time to focus beyond the noise and activities of the daily demands on our time. We may find ourselves longing for a greater awareness of God with us in the midst of it all, but asking ourselves how we can possibly add one more thing to our to-do list.

But our relationship with God is not meant to be one more thing to do. It is not meant to be just another demand on our time and energy. Rather, our relationship with God is meant to be the center from which our life's activities flow. God's presence with us is the center, the source, the light of our lives, providing the peace, the strength, the wisdom, the joy, the companionship and the purpose we seek. In his book *Making All Things New* Henri Nouwen writes:

> Jesus does not respond to our worry-filled way of living by saying we should not be so busy. . . . He does not tell us what we do is unimportant, valueless, or useless. . . . Jesus' response to our worry-filled lives is quite different. He asks us to shift the point of gravity, to relocate the center of our attention, to change our priorities. Jesus wants us to move from the "many things" to the "one necessary thing." . . . Jesus does not speak about a change of activities, a change in contacts, or even a change in pace. He speaks about a change of heart. This change of heart makes everything different, even while everything appears to remain the same. This is the meaning of "Set your hearts on his kingdom first . . . and all these other things will be given you as well."*

How can we learn to live centered in God's loving presence, in a way that allows all our activity to flow from that center? How can we experience this change of heart that will allow us to know God's presence with us in the midst of the busyness of our lives?

The purpose of this study guide is to seek answers to these questions from Scripture. We will listen as Jesus calls us to live with eyes wide open to what matters most in life, even as we entrust ourselves to God's care so we can live in the present, where God is with us, providing for us. We will hear the invitation to draw the strength we need for the day from God, the Source of all life. We will learn to open ourselves throughout the day to God as we seek God's wisdom, express our gratitude and begin to rest and rely more deeply in God's presence with us. We will explore ways of conversing with God in the midst of the whirlwind of life and come to see our day's work as a labor of love for God and as the joyful service of kneeling before all others with Jesus.

Scripture calls us to slow down, to quiet our minds and still our bodies, and to remember who God is and who we are. We are called to live thoughtfully, compassionately and humbly as the much loved children of God that we are. We are called to live in the present moment, aware of God's loving presence with us and in us, relying on God and responding in love to God and our neighbor in all we do and say.

May you come to know God's presence with you in all things. May you come to rest in God as you move through the demands of your day, allowing God to guide you, strengthen you and give you peace.

Suggestions for Individual Study

1. As you begin each study, pray that God will speak to you through his Word.

2. Read the introduction to the study and respond to the personal reflection question or exercise. This is designed to help you focus on God and on the theme of the study.

3. Each study deals with a particular passage so that you can delve into the author's meaning in that context. Read and reread the passage to be studied. The questions are written using the language of the New International Version, so you may wish to use that version of the Bible. The New Revised Standard Version is also recommended.

4. This is an inductive Bible study, designed to help you discover for yourself what Scripture is saying. The study includes three types of questions. Observation questions ask about the basic facts: who, what, when, where and how. Interpretation questions delve into the meaning of the passage. Application questions help you discover the implications of the text for growing in Christ. These three keys unlock the treasures of Scripture.

Write your answers to the questions in the spaces provided or in a personal journal. Writing can bring clarity and deeper understanding of yourself and of God's Word.

5. It might be good to have a Bible dictionary handy. Use it to look up any unfamiliar words, names or places.

6. Use the prayer suggestion to guide you in thanking God for what you have learned and to pray about the applications that have come to mind.

7. You may want to go on to the suggestion under "Now or Later," or you may want to use that idea for your next study.

Suggestions for Members of a Group Study

1. Come to the study prepared. Follow the suggestions for individual study mentioned above. You will find that careful preparation will greatly enrich your time spent in group discussion.

2. Be willing to participate in the discussion. The leader of your group will not be lecturing. Instead, he or she will be encouraging the members of the group to discuss what they have learned. The leader will be asking the questions that are found in this guide.

3. Stick to the topic being discussed. Your answers should be based on the verses which are the focus of the discussion and not on outside authorities such as commentaries or speakers. These studies focus on a particular passage of Scripture. Only rarely should you refer to other portions of the Bible. This allows for everyone to participate in in-depth study on equal ground.

4. Be sensitive to the other members of the group. Listen attentively when they describe what they have learned. You may be surprised by their insights! Each question assumes a variety of answers. Many questions do not have "right" answers, particularly questions that aim at meaning or application. Instead the questions push us to explore the passage more thoroughly.

When possible, link what you say to the comments of others. Also, be affirming whenever you can. This will encourage some of the more hesitant members of the group to participate.

5. Be careful not to dominate the discussion. We are sometimes so eager to express our thoughts that we leave too little opportunity for others to respond. By all means participate! But allow others to also.

6. Expect God to teach you through the passage being discussed and through the other members of the group. Pray that you will have an enjoyable and profitable time together, but also that as a result of the study you will find ways that you can take action individually and/or as a group.

7. Remember that anything said in the group is considered confidential and should not be discussed outside the group unless specific permission is given to do so.

8. If you are the group leader, you will find additional suggestions at the back of the guide.

---

*Henri J. M. Nouwen, *Making All Things New* (San Francisco: HarperOne, 2009), p. 42.

1

Live in the Present with Eyes Wide Open

Matthew 6:19-34

I stood at the kitchen counter, grinding coffee to brew a fresh pot for my family. My mind whirled with the grinder. In the midst of an already full schedule, I was managing the care of our ninety-seven-year-old widowed friend, and her needs were in a rapid state of change. My mind was spinning, trying to anticipate what to do, when to do it, how to find the resources. My mind came up blank. I couldn't figure it out. And the coffee? It turned out weak and undrinkable.

My whirling brain produced nothing but anxiety. And the work of my hands was abandoned as I left the present moment and visited the imaginary "Land of the Worry-filled Future." We are all acquainted with this land. We live there too much of the time. This accounts for a great deal of the stress and the distress we experience in life.

It turns out that no matter how worthy the cause we are worrying about, the worry is not only a waste of time and energy, it is worse. It is an activity that robs us of the awareness of God-with-us here, now, in this present moment. It blocks us from resting in God's presence and from receiving the many gifts of God's loving care and provision each moment of each day.

My whirling mind was the result of my forgetting that God can be trusted to provide and guide. My work was not to figure everything out but to entrust myself and our widowed friend to God's care, thanking God that the Spirit would show me what to do one day at a time.

GROUP DISCUSSION. What happens to you physically, spiritually and relationally when you worry?

PERSONAL REFLECTION. What makes it difficult to trust God's care for you?

What helps you trust God's care for you?

In the text for this study we will listen as Jesus instructs us to live with eyes wide open to what matters most, and as Jesus calls us out of our anxiety, back to the present where we can learn to rest and trust in God's loving care for us, one amazing day at a time. *Read Matthew 6:19-34.*

---

1. What wisdom does Jesus offer about the priorities of those who follow him?

---

2. What contrast does Jesus make between riches (treasures) on earth and in heaven in verses 19-21?

---

3. What comes to your mind when you think of "riches on earth" and "riches in heaven"?

---

4. Jesus changes metaphors and talks about our ability to see in verses 22-23. What is Jesus suggesting that we need to be able to see?

5. Once again, Jesus changes metaphors and talks about servants and masters in verse 24. What point is he making with this metaphor?

---

6. What are the subtle and not-so-subtle attractions of pursuing earthly riches, of keeping our spiritual eyes closed and of serving money?

---

7. Jesus then turns to nature to offer us a new perspective. What is he saying as he talks about the birds and the flowers (vv. 26-30)?

---

8. How do Jesus' comments in verses 25-34 relate to the what Jesus said in verses 19-24?

---

9. In verses 25-34 Jesus talks about anxiety and trust. In your busyness what anxiety do you experience?

What happens to you when you worry about the future rather than staying present to God's care in the present moment?

10. How do Jesus' words speak to your anxieties?

---

11. What might it be like to live one day at a time, with your eyes open to see what matters most while trusting the promise of God's love and care?

Thank God for calling you to move beyond pursuing false securities to valuing the kingdom of justice, mercy and love. Thank God, as well, for calling you to live one day at a time, letting go of anxiety about the future as you remember that God knows your needs and will provide for you.

Now or Later

For many of us, there are worries that lie beneath the worries of "figuring things out" or "getting everything done." These worries might be fears that God is not pleased with us, that we have to get everything right, that we are failures, that we are on our own, that we have to strive hard to earn God's favor. In a time of quiet, invite God to show you what some of your deeper fears might be. Invite God to bring healing to these fears and to deepen your capacity to trust God's love and care for you.

Daily prayer: May I live one precious day at a time with my eyes open to what matters most and my heart open to your presence with me.

2

Receive Strength for the Day from God

Isaiah 40:25-31

Most of us face multiple demands on our time and energy. We may frequently find ourselves wondering, *Where will I get the strength for what I need to do?*

Often, we answer this question by soldiering on, on our own. We push and push ourselves, sometimes until we are on the verge of burnout or collapse, ignoring our own basic needs and neglecting the needs of those closest to us in life.

Occasionally we may realize that we simply do not have the strength we need. In those moments we may, once again, and by God's grace, come to an end of our self-reliance and remember our need to rely on a power, a strength, that is greater than ourselves. These moments are often painful for us. We may see such moments as failure. But these moments of realizing that our strength is limited are gifts. They are moments of clarity, moments of truth.

We were designed by our Creator to rely on the strength of the One who is the source of our life. We were not meant to "go it alone" in life. Not on the challenging days. Not on any day. Learning to rely on God's strength each day is an important aspect of experiencing more fully the reality of God's presence with us in the midst of the busyness of our lives.

GROUP DISCUSSION. What are some of the demands or challenges that drain you?

PERSONAL REFLECTION. What might (or does) help you remember to ask God for strength each day?

In the text for this study we will remember that we are creatures, the handiwork of a master Creator, and that we were designed to rely on God for the strength we need to walk and not faint, to run and not grow weary, to mount up on wings of eagles and soar. *Read Isaiah 40:25-31.*

---

1. What title would you give this text?

---

2. What images of God does this text present?

---

3. In what ways do these images of God speak to you?

---

4. How do these images of God compare to how you tend to see or experience God in your daily life?

5. What difference might it make in the stress and busyness of your life to see God in these ways?

---

6. We read in verse 27 that people are saying, "The LORD doesn't notice our condition" and "Our God doesn't pay any attention to our rightful claims." What might cause a person to experience these fears?

---

7. What is God's response to these fears?

---

8. When have you experienced similar fears?

---

9. The text states that our strength is renewed as we "trust" ("hope in," "rely on") the Lord (v. 31). How might trusting (or hoping) in God open us up to receiving renewed strength from God?

10. What three images does this text use to describe what renewed strength might do for the one who receives it (v. 31)?

---

11. What might these three images be intended to convey?

Thank God for the promise of strength as you trust in God's powerful care for you.

Now or Later

What concerns or challenges are you facing? In a time of quiet, talk with God about your concerns. Ask God to help you to place your hope in God and entrust yourself and your cares to God.

What gifts of strength do you need at this time? In a time of quiet, invite God to be your strength today. Let yourself see yourself soaring on wings like an eagle, running without growing weary, walking without fainting.

Daily prayer: You, God, are my strength. May I soar and run and walk in your strength today.

3

Seek and Live in God's Wisdom

James 1:1-5, 17; 3:13-17

For most of us, the possibilities for being in continual motion and subjected to continual input are endless. Much of what we do may be necessary, and much of it may be good. Yet the choices we make on a daily basis to do, and go, and be in front of our many screens may be hurting us and others. We may be driven to gain status or power. We may be anxious and seeking numbing distraction. We may be feeling that no matter how much we earn or consume, it is never enough. We may be believing that we can never say no when asked to be of some service.

Our endless working to achieve status or power, our overconsuming, our numbing distraction, and even our need to please and impress are all likely centered in selfish ambition and pride. They are not likely to be centered in the loving wisdom of God.

Knowing God's presence in the whirlwind of life comes in part from seeking and yielding to God's wisdom in the many choices we make. It comes from learning when to say yes and when to say no as we seek God's loving will in our lives.

GROUP DISCUSSION. How might unnecessary busyness add to a person's distress and anxiety?

PERSONAL REFLECTION. Where do you sense that you are making unhealthy choices that create unnecessary busyness and add to your distress?

The text for this study invites us to ask for God's wisdom. It then goes on to help us to differentiate God's wisdom from our selfish tendencies. *Read James 1:1-5, 17.*

---

1. This Scripture begins by making a connection between life's challenges, perseverance and joy. How would you describe what the author is saying?

---

2. Have you experienced this connection? If so, explain.

---

3. How will God respond to us when we ask him for wisdom (v. 5)?

---

4. What does this say about God's character?

---

5. James 1:6-8 describes what many of us have experienced. We may ask God for wisdom and then fail to trust that God will guide us. Another way the text describes this is that we don't receive the wisdom we asked for, even though God is giving it generously. We may fret about "getting it right" and fail to pay attention to the guidance we are sensing. Or we may decide to go our own way after seeking God's will and way. What experience have you had with this problem?

6. Imagine for a moment what it might be like to fully trust that God really does respond to your requests for wisdom. How might trusting this affect your capacity to receive God's wisdom?

Read James 3:13-17.

---

7. How does this Scripture describe the wisdom that comes from God?

---

8. How does it contrast God's wisdom with envy and selfish ambition?

---

9. What are some of the subtle and not so subtle ways that envy or selfish ambition can add stress and unnecessary busyness to our lives?

---

10. How might living in God's wisdom help a person experience God in the busyness of life?

---

11. What wisdom do you need to ask for at this time in your life?

12. What help do you need from God and others to trust that God will give generously "without finding fault" (Jas 1:5)?

Thank God for being a generous giver whose gift of wisdom is available to you in every situation you face in life.

Now or Later

In a time of quiet, ask God to show you where you have been making choices out of envy or selfish ambition. Ask God as well for God's humble, peace-loving wisdom to guide you. Invite God to deepen your trust in God, who promises to give you wisdom generously. Open your hands and heart as you thank God and receive God's gifts of wisdom for you at this time. Write about your time of prayer and meditation.

Daily prayer: Give me your wisdom today. May I come to trust that you give wisdom generously to all who ask, including me. Help me to receive and follow the wisdom you provide.

4

Express Gratitude Throughout the Day

Philippians 4:4-9

Scripture instructs us to express our gratitude to God in all circumstances. This is an instruction that often eludes us. We find ourselves wondering, *What does this mean? Why is this important?* Perhaps if we understood this instruction as an invitation to see our lives and circumstances through childlike eyes of wonder and trust, we might get a glimpse of the gifts gratitude offers us.

In the months that I helped provide end-of-life care for an elderly friend in her home, I experienced some of the gifts gratitude provides. I experienced how gratitude kept me present in each moment, how it opened my eyes to gifts of grace and goodness, how it opened my heart to receive those gifts. As a result, I experienced how gratitude allowed me to know God was with us in the midst of the whirlwind.

My strongest memory of the gift of gratitude from this time came from my elderly friend's determination to walk to the bathroom from her bedroom, and from the way she saw each step as a gift. Each step she took with her walker was an occasion to gave thanks. "Thank you, thank you," she'd say, one step at a time.

"Thank you. Thank you," she'd say,
offering her soft spoken hymn of praise to you
with each step she took.
Ninety-seven, clutching walker,

while I held onto her,
she walked in thankful wonder
like a toddler taking first steps with glee.
Each step a gift, counted.
Walker steadied and grounded her body in motion
while her thanksgiving steadied and grounded her spirit
in the here and now flow of grace.

I lost count of how many of these short walks we took
that last sweet year of her life,
saying our thank-yous to you out loud
down the hall and back.
But they were many and enough to echo in my cells
and to raise up in me from time to time
this simple hymn of praise.

"Thank you. Thank you."
I find myself whispering to you
over and over throughout the day,
noticing how my eyes open to the outpouring
of grace and blessing in every moment,
how I feel myself carried on the current of your joy,
how I am able to use this walker of gratitude
to steady and ground my heart and mind, body and soul
in your glorious presence with us here and now.

Thank you. Thank you.*

GROUP DISCUSSION. Share an experience you have had with the power of expressing gratitude to God.

PERSONAL REFLECTION. What thoughts and feelings do you have in response to the experience expressed in the above prayer "Gratitude"?

The text for this study shows us the relationship between gratitude and the experience of peace. *Read Philippians 4:4-9.*

1. Using your own words, make a list of the instructions this text offers in verses 4-6.

---

2. What do you think it means to "rejoice in the Lord" (v. 4)?

---

3. What might it mean in practical terms to "rejoice in the Lord *always*"?

---

4. What does it mean to "let your gentleness be evident to all" (v. 5)?

How might this be related to living in joy and gratitude?

---

5. This text suggest several antidotes to anxiety. What antidotes are suggested in verses 6-7?

6. What antidote is suggested in verse 8?

---

7. How might following these instructions in verses 8-9 help bring us God's peace?

---

8. How does the list in verse 8 compare and contrast your typical daily focus?

---

9. How might following the guidelines in verses 4-9 allow you to know God's presence in the midst of the whirlwind of life?

---

10. What are some practical ways you might shift your focus to rejoicing, petitioning, giving thanks and thinking about what is praiseworthy?

Thank God for the peace that comes as we express our needs and gratitude to God.

Now or Later

In a moment of quiet, write a list of things that are causing you anxiety and another list of what you are needing and wanting in relationship to these anxieties. Talk to God about these concerns, as you thank God for God's love and care.

Take a few minutes to write a gratitude list, thanking God for gifts big and small, ordinary and extra ordinary.

For a moment, breath in the peace, calm, hope and joy that can flow from the practice of noticing and expressing gratitude for God's good gifts and loving activity in your life and in this world. How might this practice change your experience in the midst of the busyness of life?

Daily prayer: Thank you, thank you, thank you for who you are, for your healing work in my life and for your unfailing love for us all.

---

*Juanita Ryan, "Gratitude," in *Heaven At My Door: Prayers from the Journey* (Scotts Valley, CA: CreateSpace, 2013), p. 48.

5

Rest with and Rely on God

Mark 6:30-46

Scripture calls us repeatedly to rely on God and to rest with God. These activities work together. In times of quiet with God, we remember that we are limited, finite creators. We are reminded that God is God and we are not. We return to the truth that we were designed to live in reliance on God and not on ourselves.

The perspective that comes to us as we sit in quiet changes how we face the challenges in our lives. We begin to find ourselves moving through our busy days with deepening awareness of God with us in all things and a growing capacity to rest in and rely on God for the provision, strength, wisdom and peace we need in each situation.

Henri Nouwen described this interplay between resting and relying on God in *Making All Things New.*

> Although the discipline of solitude asks us to set aside time and space, what finally matters is that our hearts become like quiet cells where God can dwell wherever we go and whatever we do. The more we train ourselves to spend time with God . . . the more we will discover that God is with us at all times and in all places. Then we will be able to recognize him even in the midst of a busy and active life. . . . Thus, the discipline of solitude enables us to live active lives in the world, while remaining always in the presence of the living God.*

GROUP DISCUSSION. What kinds of solitude tend to restore you the most?

PERSONAL REFLECTION. What barriers get in the way of you finding time to rest with God? What might help you to remember to rely on God rather than yourself as you face the demands of each day?

In the text for this study we meet Jesus and his followers in the midst of their busy lives. We see them seeking a time of solitude and having trouble making it happen. We also watch as Jesus teaches his disciples to bring their limited resources to him so he can multiply them for the benefit of others. *Read Mark 6:30-46.*

---

1. What do you picture as you read the opening scene in this text (vv. 30-31)?

---

2. What thoughts and feelings do you have about Jesus' call to the disciples to get away with him to a quiet place and rest when there were so many people needing attention?

---

3. What benefit would there have been for the disciples in getting away to rest in quiet with Jesus at that moment?

---

4. What value have you experienced in finding a way to get away, if for even twenty minutes at a time, for rest and quiet with Jesus?

5. After a short time alone in the boat, Jesus and his disciples are again swarmed by a crowd (vv. 33-34). Put yourself in the disciples' place. What might it have been like to witness Jesus' compassionate response to the people?

---

6. Put yourself again in the story as one of the disciples concerned about the crowd getting hungry as it gets late in the day. What anxieties might you have experienced as this story unfolds?

- as you realized how late it was getting

- when Jesus tells you to feed the crowd

- when all you have to bring Jesus is a few loaves of bread and two fish

---

7. What kinds of experiences have you had with this kind of concern and sense of inadequacy in your own busy life?

---

8. What does Jesus do for the disciples in response to their distress about the enormous gap between the size of the need and their limited resources?

9. What is the significance of Jesus involving the disciples in providing nourishment for the crowd?

---

10. What kinds of experiences have you had with learning to rely on God in the busyness of life?

---

11. This is a story of great need, inadequate resources and of God providing in an unexpected way. What difference would it make in the whirlwind of your life to more fully acknowledge your need and inadequate resources?

---

12. We learn in verses 45-46 that Jesus did get a time of solitude and the disciples did get a time apart from the crowd. How might carving out times of solitude help you?

How might you build this practice into your life, even if you have to persist in trying to make those times happen?

Thank God for inviting you to rest in times of solitude with God and for teaching you to rely on God in the midst of responding to life's pressing needs.

Now or Later

In a time of quiet, allow yourself to rest with Jesus. Slow your breathing, release some of the tension in your body and let the loving presence of Jesus be with you like a soft light. Talk with Jesus about all that is going on in your life. Talk with Jesus about your concerns, your wonder at watching God work, whatever is on your heart and mind. Then sit quietly for a few minutes, resting in Jesus' presence. Be aware of anything you sense the Spirit saying to you.

Daily prayer: God, I ask to rest with you today, even as I rely on you to do what only you can do. I offer myself to you with all my limits, asking that you will be my Provider, my Strength, my Wisdom, my Peace today.

---

*Henri J. M. Nouwen, *Making All Things New* (San Francisco: HarperOne, 2009), pp. 79-80.

6

Remain in Conversation with God

Psalm 16

God invites us into an intimate relationship that is characterized by an open, ongoing conversation. Night and day we can talk to God and listen as God counsels and instructs us. Night and day we can practice awareness of God's loving presence. Night and day we can commune with God.

To remain in conversation with God (or return to conversation with God) throughout the day and in the waking hours of the night is to "practice the presence of God." It is a way of praying described by Brother Lawrence, who talked about being in conversation with God throughout the day as he worked in the kitchen to feed all who ate at the monastery where he served.

This practice of communing and communicating with God throughout the day and night is a vital way of knowing God in the midst of the whirlwind of life.

We may not think this kind of prayer is possible or practical. But when we understand that this is not about a performance or an attempt to meet some kind of goal, but simply the basic dynamic of responding day by day to God's invitation to intimacy, we can begin to catch a glimpse of the gift this practice holds out to us, namely, the gift of an ongoing, vital, personal relationship with the living God who is with us always.

Thomas Kelly says this about the prayer of communion:

> Deep within us all there is an amazing inner sanctuary of the soul, a holy place, a Divine Center, a speaking Voice, to which we may continuously return. Eternity is in our hearts, pressing upon our time-torn lives, warming us with intimations of an astounding destiny, calling us home unto Itself. Yielding to these persuasions, gladly committing ourselves in body and soul, utterly and completely, to the Light Within, is the beginning of true life. . . .
>
> How, then, shall we lay hold of that Life and Power, and live the life of prayer without ceasing? By quiet, persistent practice in turning all our being, day and night, in prayer and inward worship and surrender, toward Him who calls in the deeps for our souls. . . .
>
> One can live in a well nigh continuous state of unworded prayer, directed toward God, directed toward people and enterprises we have on our heart.*

GROUP DISCUSSION. What images come to mind when you think of prayer?

PERSONAL REFLECTION. How might it change your experience of your busyness to be able to remain in (or return to) conversation with God throughout the day and night?

In this study we will listen as the psalmist describes his relationship with God. It is a relationship characterized by communing with God throughout the day and during the waking hours of the night. *Read Psalm 16.*

---

1. What title would you give this psalm?

---

2. Make a list of all the ways the psalmist describes God.

3. How does this description of God compare or contrast to how you see God?

---

4. What difference might it make in our lives to see God in the ways the psalmist sees God?

---

5. This psalm describes a dynamic relationship between the psalmist and God. What actions does the psalmist take in this relationship?

---

6. What actions does God take?

---

7. What might it mean for God to counsel us (v. 7)?

---

8. What gifts does the psalmist describe that have come from his relationship with God?

9. In what ways does this description of the psalmist's relationship with God and the gifts that come from it mirror some of your experience?

---

10. What might the psalmist mean in verse 8 when he says, "I keep my eyes always on the LORD"?

---

11. What might this mean in your own life?

---

12. What are some practical ways that you might do this?

Thank God, who is with you always, for offering to counsel you and instruct you throughout the day and night.

Now or Later

Read and meditate on Psalm 63:1-8. Write about your reflections.

Write a psalm of your own, describing how you have come to see and experience God's loving presence in your life and describing how these experiences have affected your life.

Daily prayer: Lord, keep me in ongoing conversation with you today. May I share my thoughts and concerns and gratitude with you and listen to your counsel and instruction.

---

*Thomas Kelly, *A Testament of Devotion* (New York: Harper Collins, 1941), pp. 3, 11, 98.

7

Labor in Love

Colossians 2:6, 20-23; 3:1-17

When we entrust our lives to God, we are, in effect, offering our lives to God. In doing so, we invite God to transform us from our selfish ways to the way of self-giving love. That is, we give ourselves to God so that God can remake us into the image of our Creator.

This is the life that Jesus lived. It is a life of surrender to the God who is love. Jesus calls us to let go of our greed and our self-serving behavior. Jesus empowers us to live instead a life of love as we rely on God's strength, wisdom and help. In this new way of life, all we are and all we do are gifts received and gifts given to God.

In this way, our busy lives are made new. Whatever was driven by selfish ambition, pride or greed (including good deeds and religious activities) is let go. All that is centered in God's heart—compassion, kindness, humility, gentleness, patience and forgiveness—is pursued and undertaken as if we were doing it all for the One who loves us beyond telling.

All our words and deeds take on this singular focus. So that "whatever [we] do, whether in word or deed, [we] do it all in the name of the Lord Jesus, giving thanks to God the Father through him" (Col 3:17).

GROUP DISCUSSION. How would you define or describe *compassion*, *kindness*, *humility* and *gentleness*?

PERSONAL REFLECTION. What do you see as your typical motivation or focus for doing what you do?

In the text for this study we will explore what it might mean to let our activity become a labor of love and gratitude for God. *Read Colossians 2:6, 20-23; 3:1-17.*

---

1. As you look over the entire text, ask yourself how it describes what it might mean that our "life is now hidden with Christ" (Col 3:3)?

---

2. Describe and summarize the contrast Colossians 3:1-17 draws between the "old self" and the "new self."

---

3. What other phrases might be used to describe what is being said in verses 5-9 when it instructs the reader to "put to death" and to "rid yourself" of the characteristics of the "old self"?

---

4. What might it mean to "clothe yourself" in the qualities of the "new self"?

---

5. What is verse 11 saying?

Why is this significant to the new way of life in Christ?

6. Imagine meeting someone who displays the qualities described in verses 10-17. What might it be like to be in close relationship with a person with these qualities?

---

7. What might it be like to live day to day with qualities of character described in verses 10-17?

---

8. This text is telling us that to be "clothed" in the characteristics described in verses 10-17 is to be made into the image of our Creator. What impact does it have on you to see God in this way?

---

9. Read verse 17 again. What does this mean?

How might it change your experience of your busy life to "do it all in the name of the Lord Jesus, giving thanks to God the Father through him"?

---

10. In previous studies we have been exploring our need to ask God to be our Provider, Strength, Wisdom and Peace as we rest in and rely on God, and as we remain in conversation with God. How might this way of living help us to let go of the "old self" and put on the "new self"?

Thank God that all you do and say can be done as a labor of love for God.

Now or Later

In a time of quiet, invite God to show you where you are living from the "old self." Ask God, as well, to give you glimpses of how your life might change if you let go of these old hurtful and destructive ways. Make a note of what you sense God is showing you.

As you continue in quiet, ask God where you need to clothe yourself in the "new self." Then let yourself see Jesus clothing you in garments of compassion, kindness, humility, gentleness, patience and forgiveness. Invite God to show you how your life might change day-to-day as you put on these new clothes. Make a note of what you sense God is showing you.

Make a list of some of the tasks, responsibilities and challenges you are facing. Offer these activities as a gift of love and gratitude to God, asking for God's help, strength, wisdom and peace as you labor in love for God.

Daily prayer: Lord, all I do and all I say today, I offer in love and gratitude to you. May all be done as a labor of love for you.

8

Serve with Joy

John 13:1-17; 15:9-12

The Gospel of John records some of Jesus' most intimate moments with his disciples—moments that took place just hours before Jesus was arrested and crucified. They were moments in which Jesus demonstrated and taught his disciples, once again, about the joy of loving and serving others.

The story begins with Jesus, who "loved [his own] to the end," expressing his love by kneeling before each of his disciples in humble service. He did what only a servant would have done. He disrobed, wrapped a towel around his waist, poured water into a basin and washed each one's feet.

Jesus shared his heart in those moments, saying, in essence: "I love you. In the same tender, unshakeable way that God the Father loves me, I love you. This reality is the foundation for all of life. This reality is the source of joy. You are loved. Receive this love. Rest in this love. Stay close to me and to my love for you."

Jesus continued by calling his disciples to love and serve others.

It is helpful to notice the order of this teaching. First, we are told that we are loved. Then we are told to remain in the reality of that love. And then we are called to love each other. First, we allow Jesus to kneel before us; we receive his gift of intimate love for us. Then, we respond to Jesus' call to join him in kneeling in joyful service to all others.

As we begin to take in God's love and rest in that love, we begin to change. We begin to see others as God sees them, through eyes of love. We also begin to see each task and challenge that lies before us as an opportunity to remain in God's love, drawing strength and wisdom from God in order to joyfully give of ourselves to others.

GROUP DISCUSSION. Think of someone you know or have encountered who joyfully gave of themselves to serve and love others. What was it like to be with him or her?

PERSONAL REFLECTION. Think of a time when you found yourself joyful about serving someone. Describe the experience.

In the text for this study we watch and listen to some of the last moments Jesus had with his disciples before his death. In these fleeting moments he demonstrated his love for them and reminded them that the one commandment he was leaving them was to love and serve others. *Read John 13:1-17.*

---

1. What was on Jesus' heart and mind at this time in his life (see vv. 1-3)?

---

2. What was the significance of Jesus' act of washing his disciples' feet?

---

3. Notice that Jesus knows who is going to betray him (v. 2), but his love and his act of humble service included all his disciples. What does this tell us about the nature of Jesus' love and the love of God the Father?

4. Describe what happens in the interchange between Peter and Jesus (vv. 8-10).

---

5. In what ways do you relate to Peter's reaction to Jesus kneeling before him as a humble, loving servant?

---

6. Why was it so important to Jesus that Peter and the others received this gift of love from him?

---

7. Jesus instructed his disciples to do what he had just done for others. What things might be comparable to this act of washing others' feet?

---

8. Jesus promises blessing when we serve others in love. What blessings often come out of acts of service?

Read John 15:9-12.

---

9. What connection do you see between Jesus' instructions in chapter 13 and the command he gives in this portion of chapter 15?

10. This text suggests that there is a direct connection between "remaining in God's love," loving others and experiencing joy. How would you describe the relationship between these three realities?

---

11. How might the focus on being loved, and loving and serving others, affect the way you experience the demands and challenges of your day?

Thank God for Jesus' love and joyful service toward you and toward all others. Ask God to give you the grace to follow Jesus in living a life of loving, joyful service for others.

Now or Later

In a time of quiet, put yourself in the story as one of Jesus' disciples. Let yourself see Jesus kneeling before you to wash your feet. Notice your responses to Jesus. Notice the effect Jesus' actions have on you. Make a note of what this experience was like.

In a time of quiet, listen as Jesus says to you, "I love you. I love you with the same tender, intimate, powerful, gentle love that my Father loves me. Live your life from this love. Let the reality of my love for you be the center of all you do and say. Love and serve others from this center. This is the essence of life. This is the source of joy." Make a note of what it is like for you to hear these words of love and joy from Jesus.

Daily prayer: Lord, you kneel before me in love and joy. Help me take this in. Help me move past my instinct to refuse you. May I receive your love for me. And may I be your love for others today.

Leader's Notes

MY GRACE IS SUFFICIENT FOR YOU. (2 COR 12:9)

Leading a Bible discussion can be an enjoyable and rewarding experience. But it can also be *scary*—especially if you've never done it before. If this is your feeling, you're in good company. When God asked Moses to lead the Israelites out of Egypt, he replied, "O Lord, please send someone else to do it!" (Ex 4:13). It was the same with Solomon, Jeremiah and Timothy, but God helped these people in spite of their weaknesses, and he will help you as well.

You don't need to be an expert on the Bible or a trained teacher to lead a Bible discussion. The idea behind these inductive studies is that the leader guides group members to discover for themselves what the Bible has to say. This method of learning will allow group members to remember much more of what is said than a lecture would.

These studies are designed to be led easily. As a matter of fact, the flow of questions through the passage from observation to interpretation to application is so natural that you may feel that the studies lead themselves. This study guide is also flexible. You can use it with a variety of groups—student, professional, neighborhood or church groups. Each study takes forty-five to sixty minutes in a group setting.

There are some important facts to know about group dynamics and encouraging discussion. The suggestions listed below should enable you to effectively and enjoyably fulfill your role as leader.

Preparing for the Study

1. Ask God to help you understand and apply the passage in your own life. Unless this happens, you will not be prepared to lead others. Pray too for the various members of the group. Ask God to open your hearts to the message of his Word and motivate you to action.

2. Read the introduction to the entire guide to get an overview of the entire book and the issues which will be explored.

3. As you begin each study, read and reread the assigned Bible passage to familiarize yourself with it.

4. This study guide is based on the New International Version of the Bible. It will help you and the group if you use this translation as the basis for your study and discussion.

5. Carefully work through each question in the study. Spend time in meditation and reflection as you consider how to respond.

6. Write your thoughts and responses in the space provided in the study guide. This will help you to express your understanding of the passage clearly.

7. It might help to have a Bible dictionary handy. Use it to look up any unfamiliar words, names or places. (For additional help on how to study a passage, see chapter five of *How to Lead a LifeGuide Bible Study,* InterVarsity Press.)

8. Consider how you can apply the Scripture to your life. Remember that the group will follow your lead in responding to the studies. They will not go any deeper than you do.

9. Once you have finished your own study of the passage, familiarize yourself with the leader's notes for the study you are leading. These are designed to help you in several ways. First, they tell you the purpose the study guide author had in mind when writing the study. Take time to think through how the study questions work together to accomplish that purpose. Second, the notes provide you with additional background information or suggestions on group dynamics for various questions. This information can be useful when people have difficulty understanding or answering a question. Third, the leader's notes can alert you to potential problems you may encounter during the study.

10. If you wish to remind yourself of anything mentioned in the leader's notes, make a note to yourself below that question in the study.

Leading the Study

1. Begin the study on time. Open with prayer, asking God to help the group to understand and apply the passage.

2. Be sure that everyone in your group has a study guide. Encourage the group to prepare beforehand for each discussion by reading the introduction to the guide and by working through the questions in the study.

3. At the beginning of your first time together, explain that these studies are meant to be discussions, not lectures. Encourage the members of the group to participate. However, do not put pressure on those who may be hesitant to speak during the first few sessions. You may want to suggest the following guidelines to your group.

☐ Stick to the topic being discussed.

☐ Your responses should be based on the verses which are the focus of the discussion and not on outside authorities such as commentaries or speakers.

☐ These studies focus on a particular passage of Scripture. Only rarely should you refer to other portions of the Bible. This allows for everyone to participate in in-depth study on equal ground.

☐ Anything said in the group is considered confidential and will not be discussed outside the group unless specific permission is given to do so.

☐ We will listen attentively to each other and provide time for each person present to talk.

☐ We will pray for each other.

4. Have a group member read the introduction at the beginning of the discussion.

5. Every session begins with a group discussion question. The question or activity is meant to be used before the passage is read. The question introduces the theme of the study and encourages group members to begin to open up. Encourage as many members as possible to participate, and be ready to get the discussion going with your own response.

This section is designed to reveal where our thoughts or feelings need to be transformed by Scripture. That is why it is especially important not to read the passage before the discussion question is asked. The passage will tend to color the honest reactions people would otherwise give because they are, of course, supposed to think the way the Bible does.

You may want to supplement the group discussion question with an icebreaker to help people to get comfortable. See the community section of *Small Group Idea Book* for more ideas.

You also might want to use the personal reflection question with your group. Either allow a time of silence for people to respond individually or discuss it together.

6. Have a group member (or members if the passage is long) read aloud the passage to be studied. Then give people several minutes to read the passage again silently so that they can take it all in.

7. Question 1 will generally be an overview question designed to briefly survey the passage. Encourage the group to look at the whole passage, but try to avoid getting sidetracked by questions or issues that will be addressed later in the study.

8. As you ask the questions, keep in mind that they are designed to be used just as they are written. You may simply read them aloud. Or you may prefer to express them in your own words.

There may be times when it is appropriate to deviate from the study guide. For example, a question may have already been answered. If so, move on to the next question. Or someone may raise an important question not covered in the guide. Take time to discuss it, but try to keep the group from going off on tangents.

9. Avoid answering your own questions. If necessary, repeat or rephrase them until they are clearly understood. Or point out something you read in the leader's notes to clarify the context or meaning. An eager group quickly becomes passive and silent if they think the leader will do most of the talking.

10. Don't be afraid of silence. People may need time to think about the question before formulating their answers.

11. Don't be content with just one answer. Ask, "What do the rest of you think?" or "Anything else?" until several people have given answers to the question.

12. Acknowledge all contributions. Try to be affirming whenever possible. Never reject an answer. If it is clearly off-base, ask, "Which verse led you to that conclusion?" or again, "What do the rest of you think?"

13. Don't expect every answer to be addressed to you, even though this will probably happen at first. As group members become more at ease, they will begin to truly interact with each other. This is one sign of healthy discussion.

14. Don't be afraid of controversy. It can be very stimulating. If you don't resolve an issue completely, don't be frustrated. Move on and keep it in mind for later. A subsequent study may solve the problem.

15. Periodically summarize what the group has said about the passage. This helps to draw together the various ideas mentioned and gives continuity to the study. But don't preach.

16. At the end of the Bible discussion you may want to allow group members a time of quiet to work on an idea under "Now or Later." Then discuss what you experienced. Or you may want to encourage group members to work on these ideas between meetings. Give an opportunity during the session for people to talk about what they are learning.

17. Conclude your time together with conversational prayer, adapting the prayer suggestion at the end of the study to your group. Ask for God's help in following through on the commitments you've made.

18. End on time.

Many more suggestions and helps are found in *How to Lead a Life-Guide Bible Study*.

Components of Small Groups

A healthy small group should do more than study the Bible. There are four components to consider as you structure your time together.

Nurture. Small groups help us to grow in our knowledge and love of God. Bible study is the key to making this happen and is the foundation of your small group.

Community. Small groups are a great place to develop deep friendships with other Christians. Allow time for informal interaction before and after each study. Plan activities and games that will help you get to know each other. Spend time having fun together going on a picnic or cooking dinner together.

Worship and prayer. Your study will be enhanced by spending time praising God together in prayer or song. Pray for each other's needs and keep track of how God is answering prayer in your group. Ask God to help you to apply what you are learning in your study.

Outreach. Reaching out to others can be a practical way of applying what you are learning, and it will keep your group from becoming self-focused. Host a series of evangelistic discussions for your friends or neighbors. Clean up the yard of an elderly friend. Serve at a soup kitchen together, or spend a day working on a Habitat house.

Many more suggestions and helps in each of these areas are found in *Small Group Idea Book*. Information on building a small group can be found in *Small Group Leaders' Handbook* and *The Big Book on Small Groups* (both from InterVarsity Press). Reading through one of these books would be worth your time.

Study 1. Live in the Present with Eyes Wide Open. Matthew 6:19-34.

Purpose: To open our eyes to what matters most in life and to learn the value of living in the present, trusting in God's care in this midst of the challenges and demands of life.

Question 1. The wisdom Jesus offers is that our hearts (our affection and attention) are tied to what we treasure most. So if material riches (and all things that feed our pride or ego) are what matter most to us, our attention and affection will be on acquiring and protecting them. But if spiritual riches are what matter most to us, that is where our attention and affection will be focused. Jesus is not negating the created world here. He is not negating the value of our physical world or our physical selves. He is talking about what we treasure—about our hearts' desires. He is talking about the wisdom of treasuring God's kingdom of love, justice and mercy (spiritual values) rather than treasuring accumulation of all that feeds our selfish ambition and pride.

Question 2. Jesus contrasts material riches with spiritual riches by reminding us that material riches are temporary, whereas spiritual riches are lasting. Even though material riches are tangible and seem like the "real deal," Jesus reminded his listeners that material riches are fleeting and therefore are not what has true value.

Question 3. Encourage participants to reflect on specific kinds of earthly riches and specific kinds of heavenly riches.

Earthly riches would certainly include material wealth or financial well-being. But it could also include anything we pursue in order to increase our sense of value in our eyes, in other people's eyes or in God's eyes. It might also include anything we pursue to gain a sense of security. So it might include chasing after various forms of success or power or status.

Heavenly riches would not be born from greed, self-service, self-reliance and self-promotion. Rather, these riches would flow out of our growing capacity to receive and trust God's unfailing love and our response of love to God and to others.

Question 4. Jesus is saying that it is critical that we open our spiritual eyes to let the light in so we can see the reality of the unseen spiritual world and all that matters most. If we do not open our eyes, we will live in the dark about what is important and what is real in life.

Question 5. In the metaphor about servants and masters, Jesus is clear that we cannot serve money and God at the same time. This does not mean that we cannot earn a living for ourselves or our families. It means that we cannot seek money like it is a god—acting as if money is the source of our security or value. Jesus is calling us to let God be God of our lives, to live in the truth that God is our hope and security. Jesus is reminding us that we are to give our hearts to God, to give our allegiance and loyalty to God and the values and pursuits God calls us to.

Question 6. We all live with internal and external pressures to value material "success" or "security." Encourage group members to look at this honestly in their own lives.

Question 7. Jesus uses the poetry of the simplicity and beauty of the lives of the sparrow and the lily to paint a picture of God's attentive care and provision for us. Knowing God's loving care for us frees us from lives consumed by anxiety. We do not have to worry; we can trust our Provider. We can rely on God. God wants us to give up self-reliance and live in reliance on our Maker. This frees us to remember and pursue what truly matters.

Question 8. Taken as a whole, this text in Matthew 6 is telling us that it is possible to (1) chase after treasures that have no value, (2) walk through life blind to God's presence and care, and (3) serve financial security as if it were God. All of this is delusional. We have no power to add a day to our lives or an inch to our height. We are dependent creatures made to live not in self-reliance but in reliance on our Maker. Too often we try to figure things out on our own and spend time and energy worrying about things out of our control, while the One who cares for the sparrows and the lilies is longing to care for us.

Question 10. Encourage participants to reflect on the freedom that can come from taking in the wisdom and hope Jesus offers as he calls us to see and pursue what truly matters in life, and as we rely on God to care and provide for us.

Question 11. Encourage participants to reflect on their anxieties and to listen to Jesus' words that speak directly into our hearts and minds. Encourage them to imagine the peace of heart and mind that could come from living with eyes open to God's wisdom for living, while trusting God's loving presence and care with them each day.

Study 2. Receive Strength for the Day from God. Isaiah 40:25-31.

Purpose: To reflect on who God is in order to deepen our capacity to rely on God for the strength we need day to day.

Question 1. Encourage participants to look at the text in its entirety and to capture what stands out to them. There are no wrong answers. This is an opportunity to get a sense of the text as a whole. One possible title might be "The Power and Intimate Care of our Creator."

Question 2. God is the everlasting One, the Creator of all, who never grows tired or weary, whose understanding is far beyond our comprehension. God is also intimate and caring, giving us strength to soar, run and walk. Our way is never hidden or disregarded by God.

Question 3. Allow time to sit with these images of God. If you want, you could read the text out loud a couple of times with a two minute pause after each reading to let these magnificent truths sink in a little more deeply.

Question 4. Encourage participants to reflect on how we tend to forget God's power and intimate care and concern for us. We tend to live as if these things were not true of God.

Question 6. Encourage participants to reflect on times when this is especially true for them. We tend to move into places of this kind of despair when we are facing suffering of some kind. But it is also possible to act as if this were true on an ordinary day. We can all too easily live as if everything is up to us, as if God has forgotten or abandoned us.

Question 7. God's response is clear and compassionate. God never disregards us, and our lives are never hidden from God. And God clearly offers us the strength we need for whatever we are facing—strength to soar, run and walk.

Question 8. Invite participants to share personal stories of struggling with fears of being abandoned or disregarded or invisible or unimportant to God. It is likely that for some, such fears are an ongoing struggle that they may be only partially aware of.

Question 9. Hoping and trusting in God for the strength we need each day moves us away from self-reliance and into a place of seeing our need for and asking for God's strength. This, then, opens us up to receive from God the strength God desires to give us.

Question 10. These images are beautiful poetry: mounting up on wings like eagles, running and not growing weary, walking and not fainting.

Question 11. These images convey a flow of power and strength coming to us from God. Perhaps the images show us the variety of forms this strength can take. Perhaps sometimes we begin with soaring, and then find ourselves running and eventually walking. And perhaps these images suggest that God gives different forms of strength for different kinds of challenges in life.

Study 3. Seek and Live in God's Wisdom. James 1:1-5, 17; 3:13-17.

Purpose: To learn to seek God's wisdom for the many decisions of our busy lives.

Question 1. I think the following quote from another book I wrote is helpful:

> The connection between joy and grief is made explicit in a frequently misused text from the book of James: "Consider it pure joy whenever you face trials of many kinds" (James 1:2). The truth is I have never particularly liked this text. It sounds like pretending, like putting a good face on things, like some romantic, idealized

but completely impractical notion. It doesn't feel real. I have heard far too many religious people talk as if God expects us to always look happy, even blissful. But I know that the wisdom of Scripture also teaches us to grieve and to be honest.

So where does the joy come from? It certainly doesn't come from pretending or from trying to be cheerful. It seems that the joy comes from being open to seeing that something bigger than we are is happening. That our difficulties, which occur for all sorts of reasons, always hold out gifts to us. They offer to challenge us. They offer to change us.

This is how this text from James says it: Count it pure joy, my brothers, whenever you face trials of many kinds, because you know that the testing of your faith develops perseverance. Perseverance must finish its work so that you may be mature and complete, not lacking anything (James 1:2-4).

The journey to joy is like climbing a steep mountain. At least two things happen during the hike. One is that as we keep hiking, we grow stronger. We can't see it but our spiritual bones and muscles and heart and lungs grow stronger. The other thing is that as we get closer to the top, we begin to see a view that we otherwise would not have seen. We see the bigger picture.

Something else happens on the climb as well. Because the ascent is so difficult we are likely to see that we cannot do it alone. We need companionship. We need help. In the middle of struggling up the steep slope we find that we are not alone. Sometimes we are being guided. Sometimes we are even carried. By God. By others.

These gifts (stronger spiritual muscles, bigger perspectives, knowing we are not alone) all serve to deepen our faith. The joy that emerges out of difficult circumstances is that we gain a greater capacity to trust that in all circumstances we are held and safe, that we are known and loved.

Ultimately joy is about being loved. About knowing we are loved. About "remaining" (resting, living) in love.

It was in this way that the words "Count it pure joy . . . whenever you face trials of many kinds," came to be real for me. Many days I did not feel joy, but as I was given grace to persevere, joy had a way of emerging over and over again (Juanita Ryan, *Keep Breathing: What to Do When You Don't Know What To Do* [Scotts Valley, CA: CreateSpace, 2009], pp. 169-70.)

Question 2. Encourage people to feel free to react to this thought to "count it all joy" when we face trials of any kind. These kinds of texts can be used to silence our lament, our protest and our fears and distress when we are faced with trials (or a crisis in life). Joy often is something that comes after the grief, after the protest, after we have given voice to our distress and found God's comfort in the love of others and directly from the God of comfort. Encourage participants to feel free to tell the whole of whatever experience they have had that reflects this surprising outcome, at times, to our trials.

Question 3. It is good to pause and take in that God gives generously, abundantly, and that God does not shame us (or find fault in us) for our lack of wisdom or for asking directly for the wisdom we need.

Question 4. Again, pause to reflect on God, who is generous in responding to our requests for wisdom, who does so without judgment and who is the giver of every good and perfect gift.

Question 5. This portion of the text can read like a direct contradiction to the statements it follows. It is possible to read verses 6-8 and see God as one who shames us and who withholds if we struggle at all with doubt that our request for wisdom will be granted. But because the text is so clear that this is not who God is, it follows that these verses are describing a dynamic we often experience. We may ask God for wisdom, never really imagining that God will answer and will answer generously. When we are in this state we tend to fail to listen for God's guidance; we tend not to be willing to wait for the wisdom to come and instead dismiss the wisdom that we sense is being given to us. That is, when we are in this state, God gives generously and we push it away, unable to receive the gift being given by the Giver of all good gifts.

Question 6. When we are able to lean into trusting that God desires to give us wisdom and promises to give it to us generously, we will find ourselves waiting for God's wisdom, listening for this wisdom (including from wise counsel) and being able to receive with thanksgiving the wisdom being given.

Question 7. The text describes the wisdom that comes from God as marked by good deeds done in humility. God's wisdom is also pure, peace-loving, considerate, submissive, full of mercy and good fruit, impartial, and sincere (genuine).

Question 8. Envy and selfish ambition are described as resulting in disorder and evil.

Question 9. Encourage participants to explore the kinds of subtle or not so subtle ways envy or selfish ambition might be adding stress and unnecessary busyness to their lives. Selfish ambition can even take the form of feeling driven to agree to all requests for help or ministry.

Richard Foster tells a story in his book *Freedom of Simplicity* about the drive to please others by always saying yes to requests for help or ministry, which can be a subtle form of selfish ambition. He talks about being at an airport, exhausted, and opening up Thomas Kelly's *Testament of Devotion.* He relays how Kelly's words caught his attention: "We feel honestly the pull of many obligations and try to fulfill them all. And we are unhappy, uneasy, strained, oppressed and fearful we shall be shallow." Foster writes: "Alone, I sat in the airport watching the rain splatter against the window. Tears fell on my coat. It was a holy place, an altar, the chair where I sat. I was never to be the same. Quietly, I asked God to give me the ability to say No when it was right and good."

Foster goes on to describe how he made the commitment to set aside Friday nights for the family, and how challenging it was to say his first no to a request to speak somewhere on a Friday night. He writes, "I answered simply, 'No,' with no attempt to justify or explain my decision. There followed a long period of silence which seemed to last an eternity. I could almost feel the words, 'Where is your dedication?' traveling through the telephone wires, . . . but as the phone hit the receiver, inwardly I shouted 'Hallelujah'" (Richard J. Foster, *Freedom of Simplicity* [San Francisco: HarperOne, 2005], pp. 99-100).

This is one subtle example of how our need to please can lead to unwise decisions that add distress to our lives. But our drive to keep up with other people's knowledge or success can have the same effect, as can any choice that grows out of our need to prove ourselves or gain value in the eyes of others or of God. Learning to trust God is learning to trust in God's unfailing love for us, and learning to trust that we cannot earn our value because our value is a gift already given to us by our Maker.

Question 10. Living in God's wisdom will help us to let go more and more of the things we do out of envy and selfish ambition. These things drain us of energy and disrupt and disturb our lives as we hurt others and create chaos. Living in God's wisdom helps us make humble choices that lead to greater peace in our lives and in our relationships, as the example from Richard Foster in the note from question 9 demonstrates.

Study 4. Express Gratitude Throughout the Day. Philippians 4:4-9.
Purpose: To experience God's peace in our busyness through the practice of gratitude.

Question 1. In the NIV the text tells us to "rejoice in the Lord always" to "let [our] gentleness be evident to all" to "not be anxious" but instead "in every situation, by prayer and petition, with thanksgiving, present [our] requests to God." Invite the group to put each of these principles into everyday language.

Question 2. This is a phrase that is used often in the New Testament letters to the churches. Perhaps it can be understood in the context of a love relationship. When we meet someone who loves us, delights in us, values us and wants to spend time with us, we often find ourselves responding in joyful love. Perhaps what is being said here is, "Let yourself experience and keep experiencing the joy of knowing yourself loved and valued by God. Live in the joy of this love."

Question 3. Invite group members to share practices that have helped them to keep coming back to the joy of being loved and valued by God.

Possible practices might include (1) meditating on God's unfailing love and goodness, or on Scriptures like Isaiah 40:25-31, which we looked at in the second study, (2) writing daily gratitude lists, (3) singing hymns of praise or thanksgiving, (4) regularly affirming (quietly in our hearts and minds, or out loud in our homes or cars) that we rejoice in God's unfailing love, tender mercies, power and beauty, saving grace, and intimate care—allowing the joy of who God is to set our hearts singing and our feet dancing.

Question 4. To the degree that we know ourselves to be loved, we let go of competing with others or with endlessly striving to prove ourselves to God or to others. Instead, we are able to live from a place of resting in God's love and of growing in our awareness of God's love for all others. This generates a deep sense of gratitude to God for our life and for others, and it leaves us tender hearted, humble and gentle in our interactions and in our relationships.

Question 5. If we slow this text down, we can see it is inviting us (1) to recognize when we are anxious, (2) to think of our anxiety as a reminder to pray, (3) to tell God about our anxiety and what we are needing and (4) to do so with the gratitude that comes as we remember that God cares about us and loves us with a tender, powerful love.

Questions 6-7. The text in verses 8-9 instructs us to pay attention to what we are allowing ourselves to focus on. We are called to stop focusing on the noise and negativity of the news media, or on our resentments and fantasies of retaliation, or on other destructive thoughts. Instead, we are called to reflect on whatever is true, noble, right, pure, lovely, admirable, excellent and praiseworthy.

Question 8. Encourage group members to reflect on the effect of all the negative things we can get caught up in and to imagine what it might be like to remember God's light and love and presence with us in all things. Encourage the group to imagine what it would be like to focus much more on who God is and on the ways God is at work in this world—bringing life out of death, redeeming what is lost and healing what is broken. This practice of noticing the loving activity of God in our world is the practice of gratitude. It is the practice of focusing and finding joy in the many gifts being given and in the Giver of every good and perfect gift.

Question 9. Encourage participants to look honestly at the images and stories they frequently focus on and to reflect on how their daily focus affects them physically, emotionally and spiritually.

Question 10. The peace and joy that comes from God is a deep and ongoing reminder of God with us in all of life.

Study 5. Rest with and Rely on God. Mark 6:30-46.

Purpose: To see the value of solitude and rest in learning to rely on God in the midst of the whirlwind of life.

Question 1. Encourage participants to put themselves in the scene. The disciples are excited to have time with Jesus to debrief all that they have just experienced as they went out to teach and heal. But they could not get a moment with Jesus. The crowd was always there. The noise and busyness and demands made it impossible.

Question 2. Because the demands and needs of the people were so constant, Jesus and his disciples could not find a moment to talk and didn't even have time to eat. In the crush of all the demands, Jesus says, "Let's get out of here." This is not always an easy thing for us to do. It requires us to walk away from other people's needs, from their expectations, from their demands. It requires that we sometimes say no. And when we do, we risk people's judgment, anger and misunderstanding. Encourage the group to talk about their various thoughts and feelings in response to Jesus saying, "Let's get out of here." Explore whatever surprise, distress, relief or gratitude group members may feel in response to Jesus in this scene.

Question 3. Being so pressed by other people's demands that we (1) don't have time to connect with the people who are our support, (2) don't have time to talk things out, and (3) don't have time to eat is a setup for exhaustion and burnout. It is a setup for growing resentments. Self-care is critical to our ability to care for others. Eating, resting and spending time in meaningful conversation with people who know us and love us are life-giving and life-renewing activities. They are crucial to our ability to continue to work and serve in this world.

Question 4. Invite participants to reflect and share about times of quiet and solitude with God. What gifts have they experienced?

Question 5. In verses 30-34 we see Jesus listening to his disciples, caring about them, wanting to give them his undivided attention and to help them get some rest. We also see him being interrupted in these plans. His response to this interruption is not frustration or resentment, but compassion. This may have been a contrast to what the disciples were experiencing. Their plans had been interrupted and their needs put on hold. They may very well have felt frustrated and resentful. It is also possible that watching Jesus respond with compassion may have surprised them and spoken deeply into their own minds and hearts.

Question 6. Encourage each member of your group to put him- or herself in this story as one of the disciples. They are tired. They haven't eaten. Their plans have changed. They are not getting the quiet rest and time with Jesus that they had anticipated. They are concerned for the crowd because it is getting late and the crowd has not eaten. They may even be using this concern as a way to encourage Jesus to send the crowd away so they can finally be alone. Then Jesus asks the impossible of them. He first asks them to feed the crowd, but all they have is one small lunch offered by a child. Their anxieties might have been very high at this point. They have been raised in a religious culture of performance. And now they are being asked to perform the impossible. Fear of failure, fear of not being enough, and fear of being shamed in public are some of the fears that they might have experienced.

Question 7. Feelings of inadequacy are a common human experience. The reason for this is that there is so much that we cannot do. We are limited, finite humans. We were designed to rely on God for the big and the little tasks and challenges of life. But what we tend to do with our sense of inadequacy is to try harder to do what we cannot do.

Question 8. Jesus does not stop engaging with his disciples. He invites them to rely on him to do what they cannot do. Jesus invites them to partner with him in miracle making, breaking it down into smaller tasks, asking them to trust him one step at a time.

Question 9. Again, encourage participants to put themselves in the story. Imagine the skepticism, the uncertainty, the anxiety and the anticipation the disciples might have been feeling as they first took the small pieces of bread and small bits of fish to this huge crowd. And imagine the wonder, excitement, joy and gratitude they might have been feeling as they gather up twelve baskets of leftovers.

Study 6. Remain in Conversation with God. Psalm 16.

Purpose: To discover the possibility of remaining in conversation and communion with God in the busyness of life.

Question 1. There is no one answer to this question. It is designed to help participants survey the entire psalm for major themes.

Question 2. The psalmist describes God as a refuge, as Lord, as one who has given good gifts, as one who counsels, as one who is always present, as one who will not abandon us even in death. The psalmist also speaks of God as his "portion," which, according to H. C. Leupold, means "I have no treasure that I value more highly than my Lord." The psalmist also describes God as his "cup," which, according to Leupold, signifies that God is the "satisfying draught that refreshes and invigorates the soul" (H. C. Leupold, *Exposition of the Psalms* [Grand Rapids: Baker, 1969], p. 149).

Question 3. Encourage participants to share not only their intellectual beliefs about God but also their fears and difficulties trusting these truths about who God is.

Question 4. Encourage participants to reflect on these statements about God and to allow the possibility of these statements to be true. Encourage them to picture what impact that might have on their daily lives.

Question 5. The psalmist's actions in relationship with God include acknowledging who God is, asking God to keep him safe, delighting in those who follow the one true God, refusing to participate with those who chase after other gods, praising God, setting the Lord always before him, rejoicing and resting secure.

Question 6. God's activities, as described in this psalm, include providing security, giving a delightful inheritance, counseling, remaining at the "right hand," not abandoning in death and making known the path of life.

Question 7. The following quote regarding God's counsel is from my book *An Enduring Embrace.*

> One of the names for God in Scripture is "Wonderful Counselor." A counselor is someone who listens with respect and compassion to our questions and concerns. A counselor draws us out, helping us clarify what we are experiencing, where we need course correction and what we can do in order to change and heal and grow. Then, on the basis of this close, accurate and loving listening, a good counselor offers us advice and guidance.
>
> God, our Maker, lives in close intimacy with us. We are deeply known and deeply loved. God cares about the burdens we carry, the uncertainties we face, the needs we don't know how to meet. Throughout the day, and even at night, God invites us to seek the Spirit's counsel about all that concerns us. . . .
>
> When we move from relying on ourselves to relying on God's counsel, our minds are likely to stop spinning and fretting. When we step out of the spin and pray, "Lord, show me what to do," our minds have an opportunity to quiet. We are free, then, to wait and listen for God's guidance and counsel. . . .
>
> It is this loving, intimate relationship that heals us. It is the love of our Counselor that fills us with hope and gives us the courage and strength we need.
>
> Our Wonderful Counselor does not throw out advice from a distance. Our Wonderful Counselor holds us in loving arms, listens carefully to our heart cries, quiets our spinning minds, comforts us with understanding and whispers the counsel we need directly to our hearts. (Juanita Ryan, *An Enduring Embrace: Experiencing the Love At the Heart of Prayer* [Scotts Valley, CA: CreateSpace, 2012], pp. 232-33.)

Question 8. The gifts the psalmist describes are safety, security, provision, counsel and instruction, God's faithful presence, being shown the path of life, experiencing joy and anticipating eternal pleasures in God's presence.

Question 10. The phrase, "I keep my eyes always on the LORD" seems to describe an intentional practice of being aware of God's presence.

Question 12. Encourage participants to think about realistic and practical strategies for remaining mindful of God's presence and guidance with them throughout the day.

Study 7. Labor in Love. Colossians 2:6, 20-23; 3:1-17.

Purpose: To explore what it might mean to do all that we do as a labor of love for God.

Question 1. The text in chapter 2 describes living in Christ and being rooted in him. It differentiates this from living under the burden of human laws that are based in self-imposed worship, false humility and harsh treatment of the body. The contrast here is between being in a relationship with One who loves us as opposed to striving to achieve approval from an impossible-to-please god by following harsh rules.

In chapter 3, the author writes about having died to our old way of living in self-serving greed, and of living instead "in Christ." Life lived in Christ is described as a life characterized by compassion, kindness, humility, patience, forgiveness and love.

Question 2. The "old self" is characterized by sexual immorality, impurity, lust, evil desires, greed, anger, rage, malice, slander, filthy language and lying. By contrast the "new self" is characterized by compassion, kindness, humility, patience, bearing with each other, forgiving each other, living in love for others and living in peace.

The contrast is between living in selfish, self-serving ways that are hurtful and destructive to others versus living a life like Christ's that is based in self-giving love for others.

Question 3. Encourage participants to think of phrases that speak to them. Other phrases we might use are "walk away from," "let go of," "surrender," "admit, confess and make amends for" and "ask God to free you from."

Question 4. Again, encourage participants to think of phrases that speak to them. Other phrases we might use are "embrace," "practice," "ask God to fill you with" and "lean into."

Question 6. The character qualities described here are qualities that we are drawn to. They are qualities that make a person safe, healing, approachable and life-giving.

Question 7. It may sound attractive to think of living with these qualities, but the actual practice of living this way is often experienced as a kind of "dying to self," because it is. Self-giving love is deeply rewarding but can be experienced as costly to our egos or "old selves," which are driven to "keep up appearances," "be right," "be better than," "have more than" and grasp at security, power and control.

But this way of living ("in Christ" or "clothed in the new self") can quiet our reactivity, ease our relationships and provide a greater sense of God's presence with us.

Question 8. Encourage the group to spend some time reflecting on the implications of this. We are called to a new way of life that reflects who God is: humble, kind, patient, forbearing, forgiving, loving and peaceful.

Study 8. Serve with Joy. John 13:1-17; 15:9-12.
Purpose: To learn to make Jesus' love for us and his call to love and serve others the center from which we live our busy lives.
Question 1. We learn that Jesus knew the time had come for him to die. And we learn that Jesus loved his disciples dearly and wanted to show them the depth of his love by kneeling before them to wash their feet as their servant.
Question 2. When a guests entered a home in Palestine, they were welcomed and cared for by the host, whose servant would wash their feet. People wore sandals and walked miles on dusty roads. Having a servant wash the guests' feet was a comfort measure and a ritual of cleansing.

By taking on this task Jesus demonstrated "the full extent of his love" (Jn 13:1 NIV 1984) and the full extent of his Father's love. In taking off his outer garment, wrapping a towel around his waist, pouring water in a basin, and then kneeling before each of his disciples, Jesus took on the lowliest of tasks. In doing so, he gave each one the gift of an intimate, loving act of physical care, while honoring them by kneeling before them to serve them in love and joy.
Question 3. Encourage participants to explore this question. We are certainly reminded here that God's love is inclusive. God's love is a forgiving love.
Question 4. Peter's first response is to resist what Jesus is doing. It seems so wrong, so upside down. The Master serving his disciples. The Teacher, Rabbi, Lord, kneeling before his followers. It is more that Peter can receive.

But when Jesus responds, "Unless I wash you, you have no part with me," Peter asks Jesus to wash not only his feet but his hands and head as well.

You can feel the humor in Jesus' response: "Peter, if you had a bath already, there is no need for all of that."
Question 5. Encourage participants to put themselves in Peter's place or in the place of any of the disciples. What would it be like to have Jesus kneel in front of them and begin to wash their feet in an act of humble service? What resistance might they experience? What would it do to them to receive this gift from Jesus?

Question 6. The theme of receiving the gift of love from the Father through Jesus is at the heart of the gospel message. We often think of our part as doing, striving, giving. But our part always starts with receiving God's love. Invite participants to talk about how counter this is to how we often see our role in relationship to God.

Question 7. Encourage participants to list acts of service or of physical care and comfort that might be something akin to washing another person's feet.

Question 8. Invite group members to reflect on their experiences of serving others in love and experiencing blessings as a result. Jesus draws a direct connection between knowing we are loved and experiencing joy. Perhaps the connection has to do with the ways our hearts open when we know we are loved, and the way the fear that grips our hearts and closes them begins to ease and melt away so that we can rest in the love that is being freely offered to us.

Question 10. Again, Jesus draws a direct connection between knowing we are loved and experiencing joy. Perhaps the connection has to do with living in the flow of God's love for us and for all others. Perhaps it has to do with being free to express our truest selves, loved and loving.

Juanita Ryan is a clinical nurse with an MSN in psychiatric mental health nursing. She is currently a therapist in private practice at Brea Family Counseling Center in Brea, California. Juanita is also the author of the LifeGuide® Bible Studies Waiting for God, The 23rd Psalm *and* Praying the Psalms. *Together with her husband, Dale, she authored* Distorted Images of God *and* Distorted Images of Self. *For more about Juanita, visit www.juanitaryan.com.*

Other LifeGuides®
from Juanita Ryan

Waiting for God
978-0-8308-3146-3

The 23rd Psalm
978-0-8308-3043-5

Praying the Psalms
978-0-8308-3038-1

Distorted Images of God
978-0-8308-3145-6

Distorted Images of Self
978-0-8308-3149-4